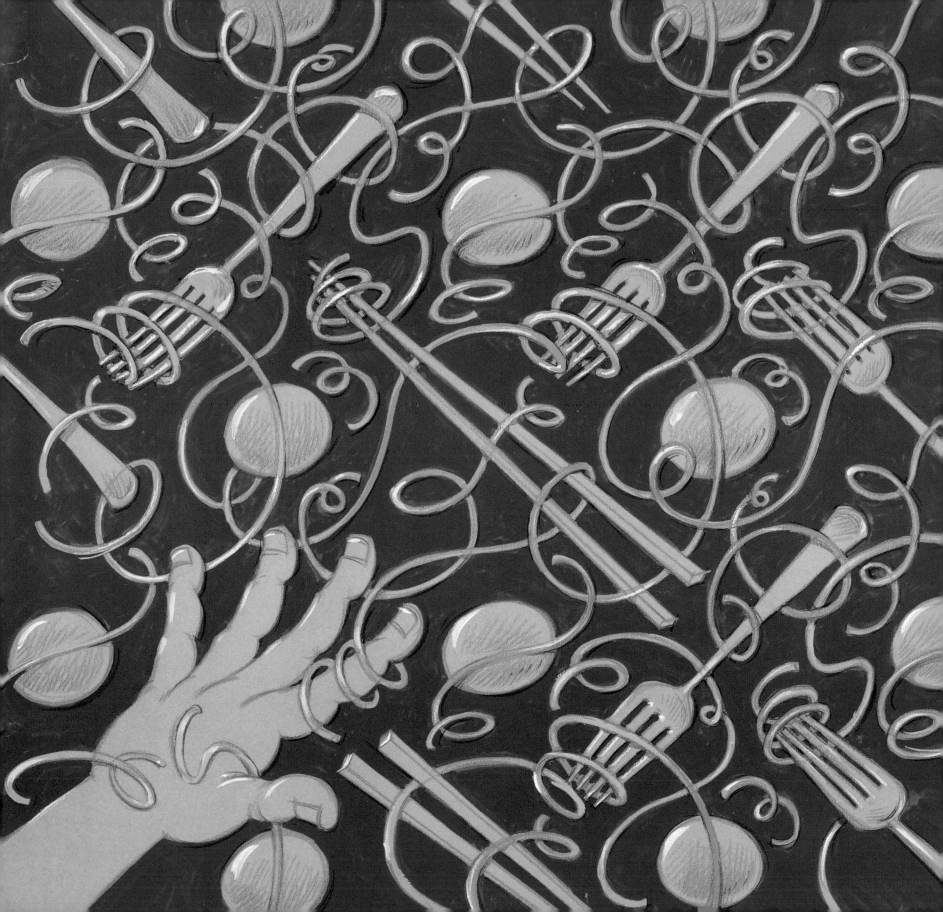

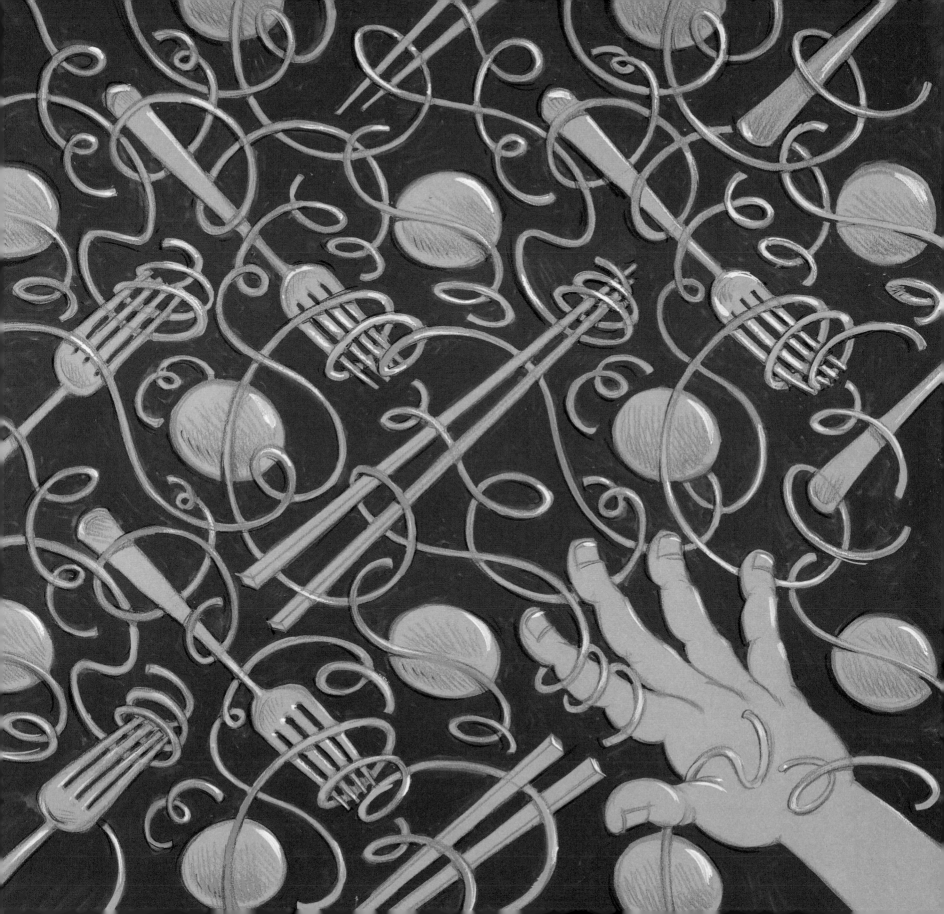

What You Never Knew About Fingers, Forks, & Chopsticks

around-the-house HISTORY

BY **Patricia Lauber**   ILLUSTRATED BY **John Manders**

Aladdin Paperbacks

New York London Toronto Sydney Singapore

We all need to eat. The first step in eating is to bring food to your mouth, but how you do this depends on where you live. In some parts of the world, people use their fingers. In other societies, they use chopsticks. In still others, they use forks, knives, and spoons for most foods and fingers for some. Each society has rules about the proper way to eat.

Fingers have always been with us. But chopsticks, forks, knives, and spoons have not. These utensils had to be invented. The inventing began in a time called the Stone Age.

Back to Nature—and also back to the Stone Age. . . .

In the Stone Age...

The name *Stone Age* describes a time when tools were made of stone. It began hundreds of thousands of years ago and ended when people discovered metal. This discovery took place at different times in different parts of the world. In a few places, there are still tribes that do not use metal.

Early people disgusting. Eat like pigs.

We very refined. Use knives, eat like humans.

Early Stone Age people ate by tearing at food with teeth and nails. But later people discovered flint, a kind of stone that often has a sharp edge.

We can only guess how Stone Age people happened to think of using flint. Perhaps…

A chunk of flint could be used for cutting meat and for scraping hides. By slashing a big chunk of cooked meat, people could make pieces that were easy to pick off. Or they could hack raw meat into small pieces for cooking.

A forked stick was perfect for cooking small pieces of meat without also cooking the fingers.

As time passed, people learned to chip flint into many shapes. They discovered how to make long, thin, pointed blades—the world's first knives.

They made containers for water out of animal skins or bark. To heat water, they dropped hot stones into the containers. Then they could cook grains.

Stone Age people also invented the spoon.

They made spoons out of shells, bone, and horn. They carved a hollow in a chip of wood, which then served as a spoon.

By 9,000 years ago, people were making pottery containers by firing clay in ovens, or kilns. They cooked stews and soups in pots and ate with spoons.

For most of the Stone Age, people moved around to find food, hunting animals and gathering plants. Nine or ten thousand years ago, some people of the Near East discovered farming. Now they could raise food and live in one place. Settlements took shape.

In the Bronze Age...

About 5,500 years ago, another big change took place. People discovered metal. Their first metal was copper. They found lumps of copper, which they could hammer and shape into objects. Next, they somehow discovered how to get copper out of certain rocks by heating them. Perhaps...

Whoops! What's that runny stuff?

I told you not to use those green stones!

About time! Stone Age go on too long.

Copper was soft, but when mixed with tin, it made the hard metal we call bronze. With this discovery the Bronze Age began. Metal knives and spoons came into use. In time, people discovered other metals— iron and steel, gold, silver.

Bamboo chopsticks of about 4,500 years ago

Meanwhile, far to the east, people had discovered a different way to eat—with chopsticks. No one knows how chopsticks were invented, but perhaps, about 5,000 years ago...

Ouch! Hot!

Didn't we already laugh at this gag?

Yes, but this time we're inventing chopsticks.

It was a great idea. Soon everyone was using a pair of sticks to handle hot food.

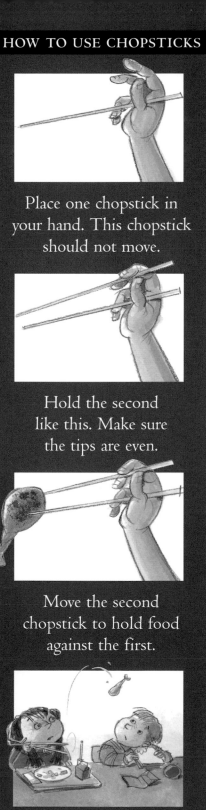

Place one chopstick in your hand. This chopstick should not move.

Hold the second like this. Make sure the tips are even.

Move the second chopstick to hold food against the first.

Do not let the chopsticks cross.

By about 2,500 years ago, when a great civilization was rising in China, the sticks had become the chopsticks we know. They were used to eat everything except soup, which was eaten with an earthenware spoon. Most food was cut with knives into bite-size pieces in the kitchen. But sometimes a whole fish or big piece of meat was served. It was so tender that pieces could be picked off with chopsticks.

Chinese spoons are flat on the bottom.

In time, the use of chopsticks spread to other parts of Asia. Most chopsticks were made of wood, bone, or ivory.

Modern chopsticks are square at one end for easy gripping and round at the other.

Ancient Civilizations—Rome

To the west, many changes were taking place as farming spread from the Near East to North Africa and Europe. The first towns took shape, supplied with food from farms. Townspeople worked at trades and in arts and crafts. Over a span of some 6,000 years, great civilizations rose in Egypt, Greece, Rome. Rich people feasted at banquets. They ate with knives, spoons, and fingers, washing their fingers in silver finger bowls and drying them on large linen napkins.

Both the Romans and the Greeks had large kitchen forks with two prongs, or tines. These were used to lift meat out of boiling liquid and to hold meat steady for carving. But there were no table forks.

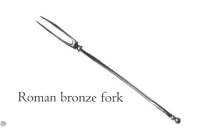

Roman bronze fork

Late in Roman times, napkins became the first doggy bags.

Egyptian bronze knife, Roman gold spoon, and Greek ladle with swan handle

Rome was the last of these three great civilizations. At its height, the Roman Empire stretched from Britain in the north to Central Asia in the east. The empire fell around the year 476, attacked by tribes from the north and east.

In the Middle Ages...

In Europe, the thousand years after the Fall of Rome is known as the Middle Ages, because it lies in the middle—between ancient times and modern times. One of the things that happened during the Middle Ages was the Crusades. These were expeditions made by European Christians, who hoped to recover the Holy Land from the Muslims. The Crusades took place between the years 1000 and 1300.

In the Middle Ages ordinary people ate plain meals. Some ate with fingers alone. Others used spoons, knives, and fingers.

The upper classes enjoyed banquets.

The knights of the Crusades followed strict rules of behavior. Their behavior stirred an interest in manners. Books of manners, or etiquette, appeared. Among other things, people learned how to behave at the table.

Readers were told:

1. An upper-class person eats with three fingers, not five.

A banquet table was set with spoons and soup bowls, one bowl for every two guests. One drinking glass was passed around the table. There were no plates. Instead, each guest used a thick slice of stale bread, called a trencher. Guests brought their own knives. The same knives were also weapons, so they had to be handled carefully. A wrong move might seem a threat.

2. A gnawed bone should never be put back on the serving platter. Lay it on the table or throw it on the floor.

3. Do not put your face in your food, snort, or smack your lips while eating.

4. Do not lick your greasy fingers or wipe them on your coat. Wipe them on the tablecloth.

5. Do not put your whole hand in the pot. Do take the first piece of meat or fish that you touch.

6. Do not blow your nose on the tablecloth or wipe it on your sleeve.

Medieval daggers

New customs arose. One paired a knight and a lady at banquets. Each couple shared food and a drinking glass.

In the Renaissance...

In the 1300s, a great age of discovery and exploration was born in western Europe. Learning was prized. The arts blossomed. The time known as the Renaissance, or rebirth, had arrived. It would last 200 years and set the stage for modern times.

Ways of eating changed.

Imagine! People used to eat off bread, not plates.

And drink from the same cup!

How refined we are!

Finally...the Fork

The biggest change of all was the table fork. Table forks had long been used in royal courts of the Middle East, but they reached the West only around the year 1100. At that time, an Italian story says, a nobleman from Venice married a Turkish princess. The princess brought table forks to Venice.

Before long, the princess fell ill and died.

Another 200 years passed before nobles in Italy started to use forks.

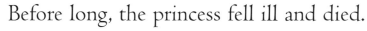

Italian Renaissance fork

In the 1500s, forks reached the royal court of France. Many thought forks silly.

Even so, forks spread to wealthy homes all over France. By the end of the Renaissance, they had reached Britain, where nobles and other wealthy people began to use them.

These early forks had only two tines. They were fine for holding or spearing meat, but not so good for peas.

The Knife Loses Its Point

Still another change lay ahead. For many years, people had carried their own knives when they traveled or went out to dinner. They cut and speared food with knives. At the end of a meal, many picked their teeth with knives. But the same knives served as weapons.

In 1669, Louis XIV, king of France, decided that there were too many stabbings. He ordered that knives were to have rounded ends. Louis also became the first person in Europe to offer guests a place setting of knives, forks, and spoons.

Swiss fork, German knife, British spoon— late 1600s

The new style of knife spread. Now that upper-class people were eating with forks, they did not need to spear their food with a knife. Even so, eating was not always easy, using a two-tined fork and a round-ended knife.

Later, a knife with a broader end made it simple to scoop up peas and other loose foods.

By the 1700s, well-to-do people were ordering sets of silver flatware for their tables. The changes called for new books on table manners. Young people were told that they should always:

American tankard, 1705

1. Use a napkin, a plate, a spoon, a knife, and a fork at table.

2. Use the napkin to wipe lips and fingers—and never, ever to rub the teeth clean or to blow the nose.

3. Use a fork for lifting meat to the mouth so as not to touch anything greasy with the fingers.

4. And never try to eat soup with a fork.

Across the Atlantic Ocean, the British colonies were not so up-to-date.

Forks! Waste of money!

I do think we should have ordered forks from England to go with the new knives.

Use your spoon.

It's hard to eat this way.

Hot!

By the mid-1700s, Americans were ordering and using forks, but they did not eat the way Europeans did. Europeans kept a fork in the left hand while cutting and lifting food from the plate. Americans ate as they had with spoons—cutting off a piece of meat, then passing the fork to the right hand. Most Americans still eat this way.

Not everybody liked to eat with a fork. Some much preferred to eat off a knife. But the fork was here to stay. New forks had three or four tines, and the tines had a slight curve. They were much easier to eat with.

American fork, 1771-1800

In the Late Nineteenth Century...

At first only the rich had sets of table utensils. Poor people ate with spoons, knives, and fingers. But times were changing. Factories sprang up in Europe and America and turned out large quantities of table utensils, which had once been made by hand. Prices fell. Almost everyone could now afford knives, forks, and spoons.

More and more kinds of table utensils were invented. By the late 1800s, there were almost too many to count.

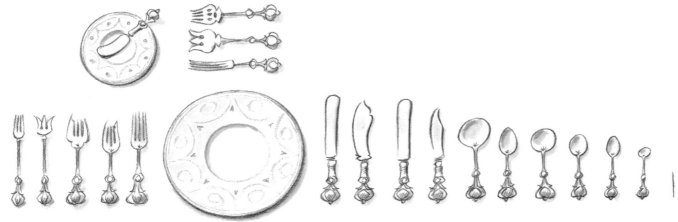

oday even fancy dinners are much simpler. At home most tables are set with only a few utensils. It's a good idea to use them and eat neatly so that other people can enjoy their food.

Some foods are eaten with fingers—but in America and western Europe, most eating is done with forks, knives, and spoons.

In Other Lands...

In other lands, you may meet people who eat in other ways. If you are a guest, it's polite to eat the way your hosts do.

Some Eskimos eat in the old way. They gather around a stewpot in their igloo, reach in with their hands, and pull out pieces of meat. Men eat first.

Some Arab families also eat with their fingers. They wash their hands, then use only the first three fingers of the right hand to eat. After dining, they wash their hands again.

In India many people also eat with their fingers. In the north, diners use only the fingertips of the right hand. In the south, they use the fingers of both hands. Both groups wash their hands before and after eating.

Japan is one of the countries where people eat with chopsticks.

In today's world, the largest number of people eat with fingers or chopsticks. The smallest number eat with knives, forks, and spoons. Each group has its own rules for eating nicely.

Some Table Manners for Today's Very Refined People

1. Cut food into small bites.

2. Do not eat and drink at the same time.

3. Do not throw a gnawed bone on the floor. Leave it on your plate.

4. Do not put your face in your food, snort, or smack your lips while eating.

5. Use fingers only for finger foods.

6. Do not reach for food.
Ask to have it passed.

8. Do not lick your greasy
fingers or wipe them on the
tablecloth. Use your napkin.

7. Chew with your
mouth shut—
do not talk and chew.

9. Sit up. Keep elbows off the table.

10. And never, ever try
to eat soup with a fork.

But sometimes it's fun to get away from it all, back to Nature…

and back to the Stone Age.

Bibliography

Barry, Ann. "The French at Table, From Celts to Now," *The New York Times*, December 4, 1985.

Braudel, Fernand. *The Structures of Everyday Life: The Limits of the Possible*. New York: Harper & Row, 1981.

Deetz, James. *In Small Things Forgotten: The Archeology of Early American Life*. Garden City, New York: Anchor Books, 1977.

* Giblin, James Cross. *From Hand to Mouth: Or, How We Invented Knives, Forks, Spoons, and Chopsticks & the Table Manners to Go with Them*. New York: Thomas Y. Crowell, 1987.

Greer, William R. "Table Manners: A Casualty of the Changing Times," *The New York Times*, October 16, 1985.

Martin, Judith. *Miss Manners' Guide to Excruciatingly Correct Behavior*. New York: Atheneum, 1982.

Needham, Joseph. *The Shorter Science and Civilization in China*. Abridged by Colin A. Ronan. New York: Cambridge University Press, 1978.

Nelson, Bryce. "Some Reflections on the Technology of Eating," *The New York Times*, August 17, 1983.

Petroski, Henry. *The Evolution of Useful Things*. New York: Vintage Books, 1994.

Stern, Philip van Doren. *Prehistoric Europe: From Stone Age Man to the Early Greeks*. New York: W. W. Norton and Company, Inc., 1969.

Tannahill, Reay. *Food in History*. New York: Stein and Day, 1973.

Visser, Margaret. *The Rituals of Dinner: The Origins, Evolution, Eccentricities, and Meaning of Table Manners*. New York: Grove Weidenfeld, 1991.

Weiner, Debra. "Chopsticks: Ritual, Lore and Etiquette," *The New York Times*, December 26, 1984.

* indicates a book written for young readers

To Mom and Dad, who encouraged my youthful obsession with drawing.
—J.M.

Artist's Note

After spending time in the library doing research, I begin an illustration with a sketch on layout bond paper using a 2B pencil. I then trace the sketch onto Arches 300-pound hot-press watercolor paper and paint the shadow and color using a combination of Dr. Martin's dyes and Winsor & Newton watercolor. The highlights are added with Winsor & Newton designer's gouache. Finally, I use a black Prismacolor pencil to redraw the sketch on top of the colors. This way, the fun of the sketch is preserved in the final illustration.

First Aladdin Paperbacks edition October 2000

Text copyright © 1999 by Patricia Lauber
Illustrations copyright © 1999 by John Manders

Aladdin Paperbacks
An imprint of Simon & Schuster
Children's Publishing Division
1230 Avenue of the Americas
New York, NY 10020

Designed by Virginia Pope
The text for this book was set in Centaur.
Printed in Hong Kong
10 9 8 7 6 5 4 3 2 1

The Library of Congress has cataloged the hardcover edition as follows:
Lauber, Patricia.
   Around-the-house history: What you never knew about fingers, forks, &
chopsticks / Patricia Lauber ; illustrated by John Manders;
        p.   cm.
   Summary: Describes changes in eating customs throughout the centuries
and the origins of table manners.
   ISBN 0-689-80479-2 (hc.)
1. Tableware—History—Juvenile literature. 2. Flatware—History—Juvenile
literature. 3. Eating customs—History—Juvenile literature. [I. Tableware—History.
2. Flatware—History. 3. Eating customs—History.] I. Manders, John, ill.
GT2948.L39 1999
394.1'2—DC21
97-17041
CIP
AC
ISBN-0-689-84412-3 (Aladdin pbk.)

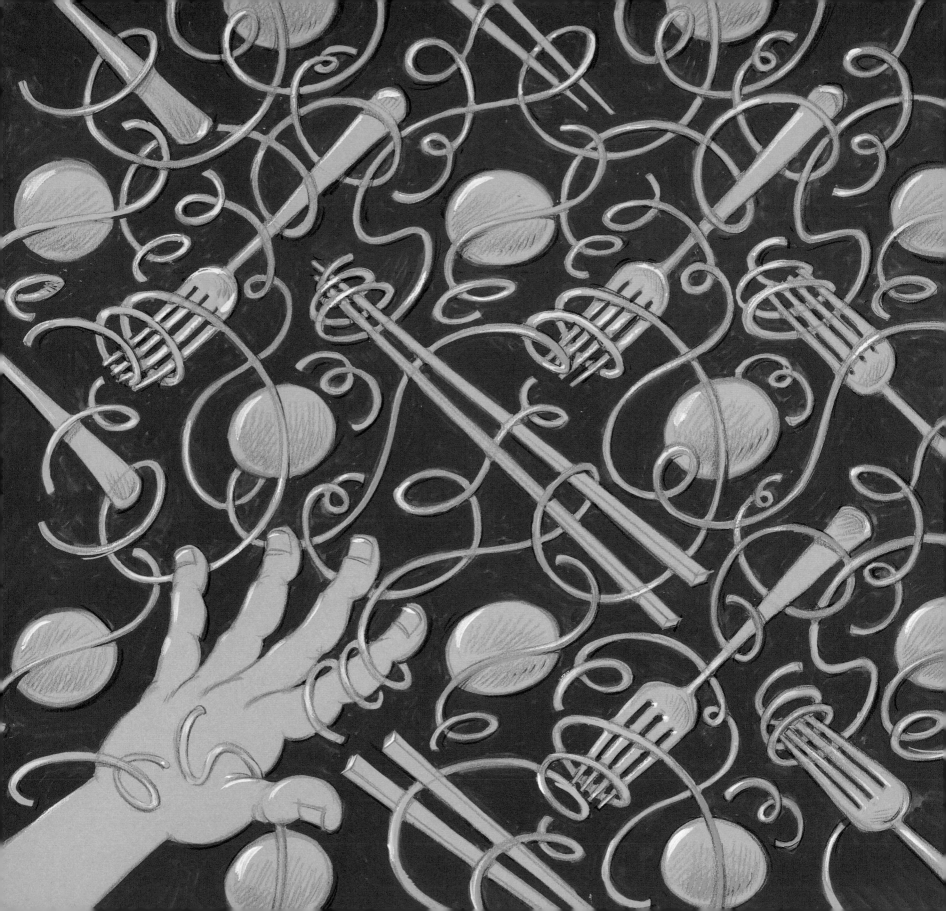

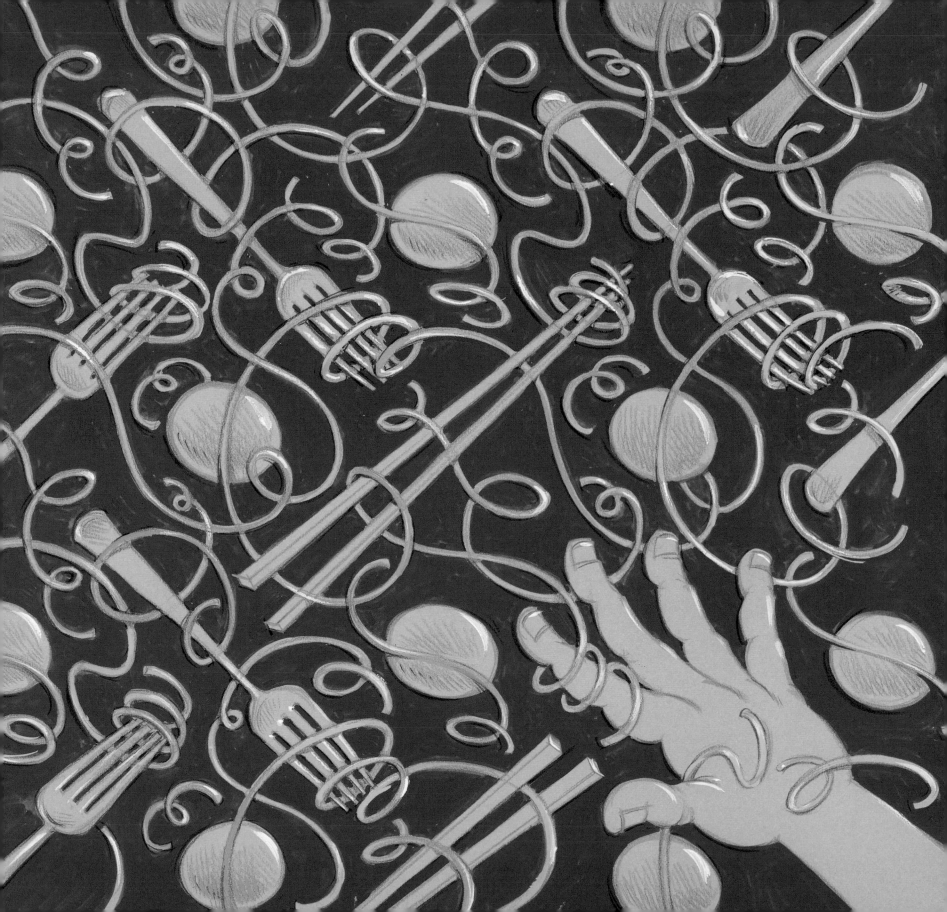